Camping

written by Kelly Gaffney

Going on a camping trip
with family or friends
can be lots of fun.
Some people like to go camping
by a lake or in the woods.
Some people like to go camping
by the sea.

First you will need to set up camp.
It's best to find a place that is not
on a hill, then your things
will not roll away.
It's also good to be near running water,
so you can wash all your things.

Next find a good place to put up your tent.
Find a place that is flat,
so your tent will not fall over.
Before you put it up,
take away all the sticks and stones
that are on the ground.

Now that your tent is up,
you can go hiking in the woods.
Make sure you stay on the path.
When you are hiking, look around,
you may see lots of new fun things.
You may see animals
and other daytime things.

At night, it's fun to sit around a campfire.
The fire will make you feel warm,
and you can cook on it, too.
Make sure you don't get
in the way of the flames.
And always put the fire out
before going on a hike or to sleep.

At night, it's also fun to go
hiking in the woods.
Make sure you go hiking
with your mum or your dad.
When you go hiking, take a torch.
You may see new animals
and other night-time things.

When it's bedtime, get into your tent.
Then get into your big sleeping bag.
It will make you feel warm
when you are reading or sleeping.
You can hang up a light in your tent
so you can read.

It's lots of fun to go camping with your family or friends!

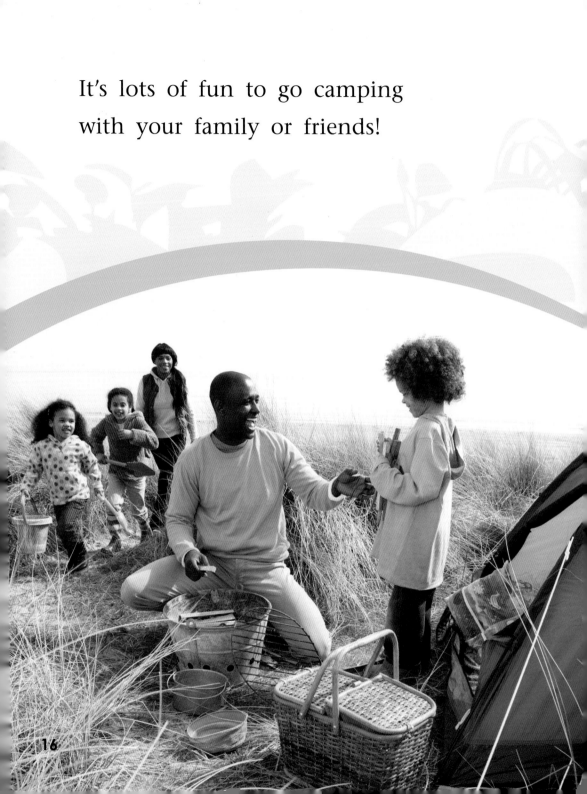